BOXER BOOKS Ltd. and the distinctive Boxer Books logo are trademarks of Union Square & Co., LLC.
Union Square & Co., LLC, is a subsidiary of Sterling Publishing Co., Inc.

Text © 2024 Boxer Books
Illustrations © 2024 Pintachan

All rights reserved. No part of this publication may be reproduced, stored in a retrieval system, or transmitted in any form or by any means (including electronic, mechanical, photocopying, recording, or otherwise) without prior written permission from the publisher.

First published in Great Britain in 2024.

ISBN 978-1-4547-1172-8

A catalogue record for this book is available from the British Library.

For information about custom editions, special sales, and premium purchases, please contact specialsales@unionsquareandco.com.

Printed in China
10 9 8 7 6 5 4 3 2 1

01/24

unionsquareandco.com

Spring Street™ Series created by David Bennett
Written by Sasha Morton
Illustrated by Pintachan
Series editors: Sasha Morton and Leilani Sparrow
Series consultant: Mary Anne Wolpert, Cambridge University

JOBS
Contents

Emergency! 6

Getting better 8

Working with animals 10

Conserving our planet 12

Spread the word! 14

Let's read! 16

Look at this! 18

Put on a show! 20

Music makers 22

IT experts! 24

We design spaces 26

We build places 28

A world of wellness 30

Time to eat! 32

Farm to fork 34

At your service 36

Travelling around 38

Working off-planet! 40

Here to help 42

Back to school 44

Spring Street

Emergency!

1 Coast guards make sure people and boats are safe at sea.

2 Firefighters work fast to put out fires and stop them from spreading.

Emergency services are the people we call when something goes wrong. They help to keep us safe wherever we are. The three main emergency services are police, paramedics and firefighters, but perhaps you've seen some of these other first responders in action, too?

1	coast guards	**3**	paramedic	**5**	fire and rescue helicopter
2	firefighter	**4**	lifeboat rescue team	**6**	police officer

Getting better

1 Doctors who are experts at treating sick children are called paediatricians.

2 Nurses care for sick people.

3 Doctors are trained to figure out why we feel unwell and make us feel better.

If we feel unwell, these specially trained people take care of us and help us to recover. There are lots of different jobs in medicine – here are a few of them. **Maybe one day you could help someone get better?**

5 The pharmacist's job is to give people the medicines that doctors say they need.

4 A midwife helps to deliver babies.

6 Surgeons perform operations to help sick people get better.

7 A radiologist scans the inside of your body to find out where the problem may be.

1 paediatrician **3** doctors **5** pharmacist **7** radiologist

2 nurse **4** midwife **6** surgeon

Working with animals

1 A veterinarian helps treat animals and gives advice on how to keep them healthy.

2 Veterinary assistants take care of animals after they've had operations.

3 Most dogs need to be walked at least once a day to stay fit and well – that's what dog walkers do!

4 Zookeepers look after the animals in a zoo – from ants to zebras!

It's not just people who need experts to keep them fit and well – animals need carers, too! All of these jobs help treat and protect our feathered, furry and four-legged friends.

5 Pet shelter volunteer staff give up their time to look after animals who need a home.

6 Pet groomers clip claws and wash and trim fur to keep pets tidy and clean.

7 A beekeeper collects the honey that bees produce in a beehive. *Buzz!*

8 Wildlife sanctuary staff care for animals in protected habitats.

1 veterinarian	**3** dog walker	**5** pet shelter volunteers	**7** beekeeper
2 veterinary assistant	**4** zookeeper	**6** pet groomer	**8** wildlife sanctuary staff

Conserving our planet

1 Marine biologists study our seas and oceans.

2 Ecology educators explain how and why we should look after our planet.

3 Ocean cleanup crews clear rubbish from the water.

Conservationists are people who want to preserve and improve the different environments that people and wildlife live in. Some parts of their job involve making people aware of problems, and other parts are all about making the planet a better place for everyone. **What could you do to help?**

4 If you want someone to plan, manage and reduce waste, you need a recycling officer!

5 Wildlife conservationists protect things in the natural world.

6 Ornithologists are bird experts.

7 A botanist is an expert in plants.

1 marine biologists	**4** recycling officer	**7** botanist
2 ecology educator	**5** wildlife conservationists	
3 ocean cleanup crew	**6** ornithologist	

Spread the word!

1 Reporters sometimes interview people live on TV!

2 Journalists investigate news stories and write about them for newspapers, online media, TV and radio.

3 Influencers show and describe the things they like doing to people watching online.

How does everyone find out what is going on in the world? From sports events to the decisions that are made by different countries' leaders, there is someone to report on every subject under the sun. What interesting news would you like to tell the world about?

4 Bloggers and vloggers use words and videos to tell us about things they are interested in.

5 Newspaper editors decide what stories and information will go in the newspaper that day.

6 News broadcasters read the news so that we know what's going on!

7 A camera operator films news or events as they happen.

1. reporter
2. journalist
3. influencer
4. blogger and vlogger
5. newspaper editor
6. news broadcaster
7. camera operator

Let's read!

1 An author comes up with ideas and writes all the words in the book.

2 Editors work with the author on the story and to make sure the text is correct.

3 An illustrator creates the pictures you're looking at now!

4 Designers create the cover and organise all the pages inside.

Have you ever wondered how many people are needed to create a book? Publishing is what happens when a book is produced, and it involves lots of people with special skills. **Maybe one day you'll have a job working on books?**

16

5 Production staff make sure the book is printed correctly.

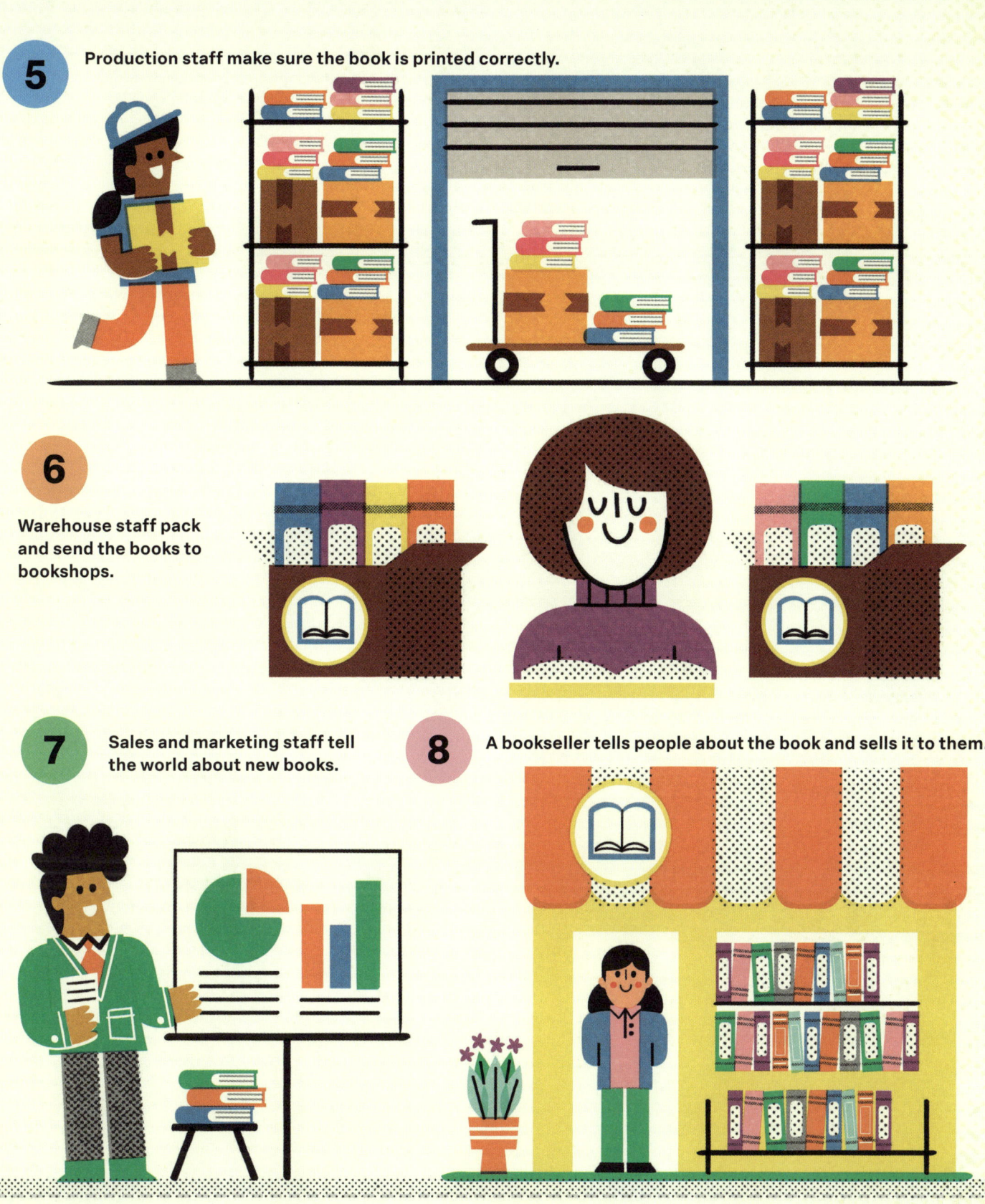

6 Warehouse staff pack and send the books to bookshops.

7 Sales and marketing staff tell the world about new books.

8 A bookseller tells people about the book and sells it to them.

1. author
2. editor
3. illustrator
4. designer
5. production staff
6. warehouse staff
7. sales and marketing staff
8. bookseller

Look at this!

1 Mural makers work BIG!

2 Painters may paint landscapes or portraits – anything can be created in paint.

3 Textile designers create fabrics for fashion designers to work with.

4 Photographers use a camera to take fantastic photos of what they see.

Artists and designers create amazing works of art that make our world more beautiful and interesting to look at. They use a whole array of different materials to turn something simple into something amazing. Which kind of artist would you like to be?

5 Graphic designers use computer software to create images and symbols to convey a message.

6 Sculptors use stone, wood or even ice to create statues.

A product designer decides what objects should look like and how they work.

7 Potters make things from clay.

1	mural maker	**3**	textile designer	**5**	graphic designer	**7**	potter
2	painter	**4**	photographer	**6**	sculptor	**8**	product designer

19

Put on a show!

1 The director on a movie set tells everyone what to do.

2 The lighting crew uses lights to create atmosphere and effects on the stage or screen.

3 A scriptwriter writes the words for the actors to say on stage, in movies and on TV.

4 Prop makers create all the things that help tell the story you see, from cups to jewellery.

Everything you watch on TV or at the movies, or see performed onstage or in the street takes a lot of different skills to create. **Which of these entertainment jobs would you be good at?**

5 Set decorators design and make a show's scenery.

6 Makeup artists have the skills to transform how people look!

8 An actor plays a character and pretends to be them onstage or on-screen.

7 Costume designers design and make the actors' clothes for the stage or screen.

1 director	**4** prop maker	**7** costume designer
2 lighting crew	**5** set decorator	**8** actor
3 scriptwriter	**6** makeup artist	

Music makers

2 A conductor keeps all the musicians in an orchestra in time so the music sounds perfect!

1 Composers write music and songs for musicians to play and sing.

3 Sound engineers help record the music in a studio and make sure it sounds good.

4 The person who introduces the songs played on the radio is the disc jockey, or DJ.

ON AIR

Our world would be a very dull – and quiet! – place without music, but there are many jobs you can do even if you can't sing or play an instrument! **Let's make some noise!**

6 A band leader is the head of a group of musicians that play pop, jazz, blues, brass or big band sounds.

5 Musicians play instruments – from small violins to very large drums!

7 DJs play music for people at parties or events.

8 Talent scouts find new musicians.

1 composer	**4** disc jockey	**7** DJ
2 conductor	**5** musician	**8** talent scout
3 sound engineer	**6** band leader	

IT experts!

1 Software designers create the different apps and programmes we use.

2 UX (User Experience) designers make using apps and websites easier!

3 IT (Information Technology) support staff help people fix tech problems.

One of the ways we work and play today is on a computer. All the things you see on your computer screen – and the screen itself – have been designed by someone. And another person needs to know how to fix things when they go wrong!

4 Animators make movies using digital technology.

5 SFX (Special Effects) teams use digital technology to make imaginary things look real!

6 Game developers create computer games.

1 software designer

2 UX designer

3 IT support staff

4 animator

5 SFX team

6 game developer

25

We design spaces

1 Architects design buildings and think about how they are to be used – homes, stores, schools and train stations.

2 Civil engineers work out how to build things safely.

Look around you. The place you are in right now was designed by someone who had an idea about how it should look and what it would be used for. Everything from its shape and size to the materials that were used was carefully thought about by these clever people.

3 Landscape architects make outdoor spaces useful and welcoming.

4 Interior designers decide how the inside of buildings should look.

1 architect

2 civil engineer

3 landscape architect

4 interior designer

We build places

1 Construction workers dig out the foundations and build the walls of buildings.

2 Scaffolders put up scaffolding platforms around buildings so workers can access higher outside levels safely.

3 Roofers put roofs on new buildings and fix damage to old ones.

Builders take the plans drawn by architects and turn their drawings into spaces to live, play, learn and work in. There is a whole team of people involved in every stage of each building project. **Have you ever seen inside a construction site?**

1 construction workers	4 landscaper	7 painter
2 scaffolders	5 gardener	8 plumber
3 roofers	6 glaziers	9 electrician

A world of wellness

1 People go to beauticians to improve the way they look.

2 *Snip! Snip!* Hairdressers cut, colour and style hair.

3 Nutritionists know all about healthy eating.

4 A fitness coach helps people stay fit and healthy through exercise.

These are some of the many people who keep our minds and bodies looking and feeling good. They play an important part in making a busy world feel less stressful.

5 Therapists talk with people to help them overcome problems.

6 Personal trainers support and coach individual people as they exercise.

7 Yoga instructors bring calm to people through special breathing exercises and movements.

8 Barbers usually cut men's hair and trim beards.

9 Physiotherapists often help people recover from injuries.

1 beautician	4 fitness coach	7 yoga instructor
2 hairdresser	5 therapist	8 barber
3 nutritionist	6 personal trainer	9 physiotherapist

Time to eat!

1 Sushi chefs use fresh vegetables, rice and raw fish to make delicious Japanese food.

2 Café chefs prepare quick-to-cook food.

3 Food truck vendors drive up to places and cook and serve food from their trucks.

Whether it's spicy food, a plate of pancakes or a burger, there is a chef for every type of meal or drink you can imagine. **What do you like to eat and drink?**

4 A baker makes bread, cakes, pastries and desserts.

5 Baristas serve up hot and cold coffee.

6 Ice cream scoopers make delicious desserts from ice cream, frozen yoghurt or sorbet.

7 Juice bar staff make healthy juices and smoothies to order.

1 sushi chef	**3** food truck vendor	**5** barista	**7** juice bar staff
2 café chef	**4** baker	**6** ice cream scooper	

Farm to fork

1 Farmers grow grain, fruit, or vegetable crops, or raise animals like cows or pigs.

2 Fishermen usually go out in boats to catch fish.

3 Much of the food we eat is collected from orchards and fields by fruit and vegetable pickers.

Farmers and fishermen have a vital role to play in making sure everyone gets enough to eat. Their produce needs to be grown, picked, packed and sent to shops for us to buy. **Let's find out who else is involved!**

4 Delivery drivers take the food from farms to places where it can be bought and sold.

5 Farm shop staff sell goods from a farm directly to customers.

6 Farmers market workers make beautiful displays of fresh produce.

7 Factory workers turn these ingredients into the food we see in supermarkets.

1	farmer	**3**	fruit and vegetable pickers	**5**	farm shop staff	**7**	factory worker
2	fisherman	**4**	delivery driver	**6**	farmers market worker		

At your service

1 Grocers sell fresh fruit, vegetables and other food products.

2 Who chooses what goes on display at a museum or gallery? That's the job of a museum curator.

3 A petrol station attendant puts fuel in people's cars.

4 Florists sell and deliver flowers.

Let's take a stroll through your town and see who's hard at work. These people help make where you live a cool place to spend time.

5 If you need to find a book at your local library, a librarian will help you.

6 Sanitation workers and street cleaners make sure where we live stays clean.

7 Cinema ushers help people buy tickets and find their seats.

8 Delivery drivers bring food like pizza to our doorstep!

9 Busy salespeople help us find things to buy in all kinds of shops.

1 grocer	**4** florist	**7** cinema usher
2 museum curator	**5** librarian	**8** delivery driver
3 petrol station attendant	**6** sanitation worker and street cleaner	**9** salesperson

Travelling around

1 Delivery drivers drop off everything from socks to food on your doorstep.

2 Postal workers deliver post and packages.

3 Let's hop in a cab! The taxi driver will take us where we need to go.

4 Long-distance lorry drivers often move items from one country to another.

Knock! Knock! There's somebody at the door! But have you ever stopped to think about all the different jobs that involve travelling from place to place?

5 Up, up and away! Pilots fly and land aircraft.

6 Train drivers take us on short and long railway trips.

7 Bicycle couriers are a way to get important items somewhere fast.

8 Removal men will take your belongings to your new home if you move.

1	delivery driver	**4**	lorry driver	**7**	bicycle courier
2	postal worker	**5**	pilot	**8**	removal man
3	taxi driver	**6**	train driver		

Working off-planet!

1. Astronauts are trained to travel in a spacecraft. Five, four, three, two, one... Liftoff!

2. Engineers on the International Space Station work 250 miles (402km) above our heads.

3. Astronomers study the universe to help us understand our solar system and other galaxies.

Some jobs are simply out of this world! Here are some roles that could take you off the Earth's surface and into a galaxy far, far away... or help you become an awesome space scientist.

4 Meteorologists study the Earth's atmosphere and oceans to predict weather patterns.

5 Astrochemists figure out what stars and comets are made from.

1 astronaut **3** astronomer **5** astrochemist

2 engineer **4** meteorologist

Here to help

1 A nursery assistant takes care of small children before they start school.

2 A tai chi instructor trains people in this Chinese martial art.

3 A music therapist uses music and sound to improve people's well-being.

Whether you're young or old, there's someone out there whose job it is to make your life safer and more interesting. **From spending time together to trying out a new hobby, who would you like to learn from?**

4 Dance teachers teach people to dance.

5 Sports coaches help people achieve their best at a sport.

6 Elder care workers look after or give support to older people.

7 Want to learn to paint, draw or create something cool? An arts and crafts teacher can make that happen.

1 nursery assistant
2 tai chi instructor
3 music therapist
4 dance teacher
5 sports coach
6 elder care worker
7 arts and crafts teacher

Back to school

1 The head teacher is in charge of the whole school.

2 Counsellors talk with anyone who wants to discuss their problems, thoughts or feelings.

3 Teachers share their knowledge so that students can develop new skills and learn about different subjects.

One of the most important jobs is that of a teacher – after all, without them, we might not even know how to read this book! Many other people work in schools, too. **Let's keep learning together, whatever job you choose!**

4 Office staff order supplies and equipment.

5 Kitchen staff prepare school meals.

6 Classroom assistants suppport teachers and look after students.

7 Caretakers keep schools clean and tidy.

1. head teacher
2. counsellor
3. teacher
4. office staff
5. kitchen staff
6. classroom assistant
7. caretaker